Super Sports Numbers

Understand Place Value

Nick Kleist

NEW YORK

Published in 2015 by The Rosen Publishing Group, Inc.
29 East 21st Street, New York, NY 10010

Book Design: Katelyn Londino

Photo Credits: Cover Al Tielemans/Sports Illustrated/Getty Images; p. 5 Jeff Zelevansky/Getty Images; p. 7 Eric Broder Van Dyke/Shutterstock.com; p. 9 (background) Chris Rokitski/Shutterstock.com; p. 9 (Cy Young) Transcendental Graphics/Getty Images; p. 9 (Walter Johnson) Underwood Archives/Archive Photos/Getty Images; pp. 11 (background), 13 (background) David Lee/Shutterstock.com; p. 11 (Barry Bonds) John Capella/Sports Imagery/Getty Images; pp. 11 (Hank Aaron), 19 (Wilt Chamberlain, Jerry West) Focus On Sport/Getty Images; p. 13 (Peyton Manning) Andy Lyons/Getty Images; p. 13 (Brett Favre) Chris Graythen/Getty Images; p. 15 (background) Chris Hill/Shutterstock.com; p. 15 (Jerry Rice) David Madison/Getty Images; p. 15 (Emmitt Smith) Donald Miralle/Getty Images; p. 17 (background) HARELUYA/Shutterstock.com; p. 17 (Abby Wambach) Patrick Smith/Getty Images; p. 17 (Mia Hamm) Shaun Botterill/Getty Images; p. 19 (background) iStock/Thinkstock.com; p. 21 (background) Shooter Bob Square Lenses/Shutterstock.com; p. 21 (Wayne Gretzky) J MIsaac/Bruce Bennett/Getty Images; p. 21 (Gordie Howe) Steve Babineau/National Hockey League/Getty Images; p. 22 Mitch Gunn/Shutterstock.com.

Library of Congress Cataloging-in-Publication Data

Kleist, Nick, author.
 Super sports numbers : understand place value / Nick Kleist.
     pages cm. — (Math masters. Numbers and operations in base ten)
 Includes index.

ISBN 978-1-4777-4666-0 (pbk.)
ISBN 978-1-4777-4667-7 (6-pack)
ISBN 978-1-4777-6401-5 (library binding)

1. Place value (Mathematics)—Juvenile literature. 2. Decimal system—Juvenile literature. 3. Sports—Statistics—Juvenile literature. 4. Sports records—Juvenile literature. I. Title.
 QA141.3
 513.2'1—dc23
                          2013038970

Manufactured in the United States of America

CPSIA Compliance Information: Batch #WS15RC: For further information contact Rosen Publishing, New York, New York at 1-800-237-9932.

Contents

Playing Sports

Do you play any sports? If you do, you know that it takes a lot of hard work to become good at them. **Athletes** spend a lot of time practicing and staying healthy so they can win as many games as possible. Some athletes are so good they hold records. That means they did something better than other athletes in their sport.

Athletes hold records for doing something more often or better than other athletes. This includes being the fastest or scoring the most points.

How do we know if an athlete holds a record? We compare their **statistics** to those of other athletes who play the same sport. Some athletes' records are 3-digit numbers, which means they're in the hundreds. These records are very big! We can use the hundreds place, tens place, and ones place to compare the numbers.

> The bigger of 2 numbers is "greater than."
> The smaller of 2 numbers is "less than."
> If the numbers are the same, they're "equal."

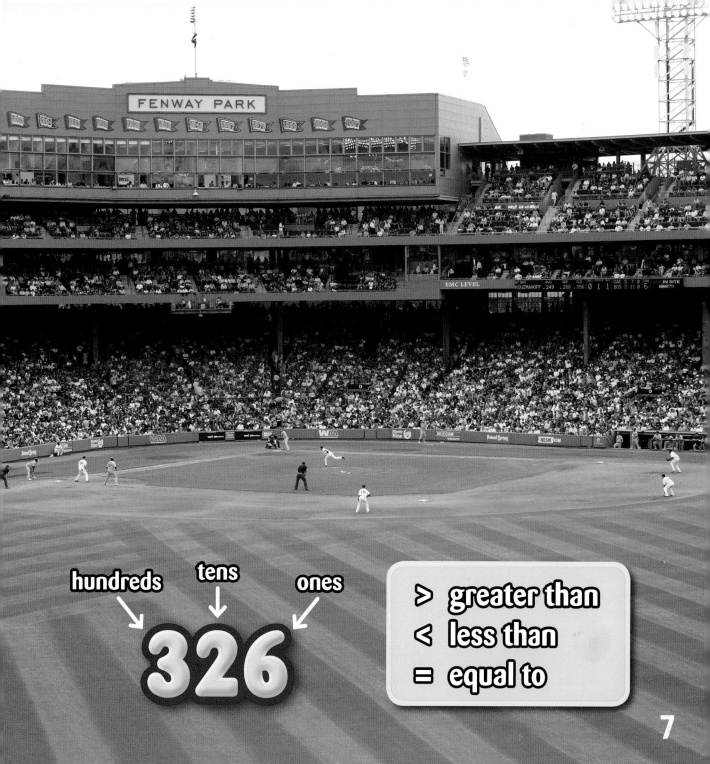

hundreds tens ones

326

> greater than
< less than
= equal to

Baseball Records

Baseball is a very fun sport. The pitcher is one of the most important players on the team. One of the most famous pitchers in baseball history is Cy Young. He pitched 511 winning games during his **career**. Another famous pitcher is Walter Johnson. He pitched 417 winning games. Since 511 is greater than 417, that means Cy Young holds the record.

You can tell which number is greater by looking at the hundreds place. Since 5 hundreds is greater than 4 hundreds, we know Cy Young pitched more winning games.

Cy Young

Walter Johnson

511 > 417

Home runs are a big part of baseball. Barry Bonds is a player who hit 762 home runs. Hank Aaron hit a lot of home runs, too. He hit 755. One of these players holds the record for most home runs. Both numbers have 7 in the hundreds place. Since 7 is equal to 7, we need to look at the tens place to find out which player holds the record.

The tens place shows that Barry Bonds hit more home runs than Hank Aaron. Do you know why? It's because 6 is greater than 5.

Barry Bonds

Hank Aaron

762 > 755

Football Records

Football is another sport with cool records. The quarterback is an important player because he throws the ball to other players so they can score. These are called **touchdown** passes. Peyton Manning and Brett Favre are quarterbacks with a lot of touchdown passes. Peyton Manning threw 491 as of February 2014, while Brett Favre threw 508. Which player holds the record?

Comparing the hundreds shows 4 is less than 5. That means Peyton Manning has thrown fewer touchdown passes so far, so Brett Favre still holds the record.

Peyton Manning

Brett Favre

491 < 508

Quarterbacks throw the ball, but other players run with the ball to score. It's hard to do, so these players must be fast. Jerry Rice scored 208 touchdowns in his career. Emmitt Smith scored a lot of touchdowns, too. He scored 175. The number 208 is greater than 175, so Jerry Rice holds the record for scoring the most touchdowns.

It's easy to compare these numbers. When you look at the hundreds place, you see that 2 is greater than 1. This shows that Jerry Rice holds the record.

Jerry Rice

Emmitt Smith

208 > 175

Soccer Records

Soccer players work hard to be the best. Two of the most famous U.S. soccer players are Abby Wambach and Mia Hamm. They're famous because they scored a lot of goals playing for the U.S. National Team. Abby Wambach scored her 167th goal in 2014. Mia Hamm scored 158 in her whole career. These numbers are close, but they're not equal! Which number is greater?

Since 6 is greater than 5, we know 167 is greater than 158. That means Abby Wambach has scored more goals in games played against different countries than any other soccer player.

Abby Wambach

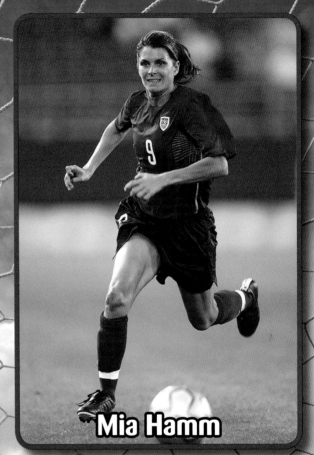

Mia Hamm

167 > 158

Basketball Records

Basketball is another fun sport. Players can score points by making **free throws**. Wilt Chamberlain made 835 free throws in 1 season. But there's a player who made more. It's Jerry West. He made 840 free throws in 1 season. Why is 835 less than 840? Look at the tens place to find out!

Both numbers have equal hundreds, so the tens place tells the answer. Since 3 is less than 4, we know 835 is less than 840. This means that Jerry West holds the single-season free throw record.

Wilt Chamberlain

Jerry West

835 < 840

Hockey Records

Have you ever played hockey? It's a sport played on ice. Players **compete** to score a lot of goals. The two players who scored the most goals ever are Wayne Gretzky and Gordie Howe. Wayne Gretzky scored 894 goals, while Gordie Howe scored 801. Which number is greater? How can you tell? The player with the most holds the record!

To compare these numbers, use the hundreds, tens, and ones places. Since the hundreds are equal, what do you look at next?

Wayne Gretzky

Gordie Howe

894 ? 801

It takes a lot of hard work to be an athlete. It takes even more work to be an athlete who holds a record. These athletes become record holders by pushing themselves to work as hard as they can. By practicing, working hard, and never giving up, these athletes have become famous for being the best.

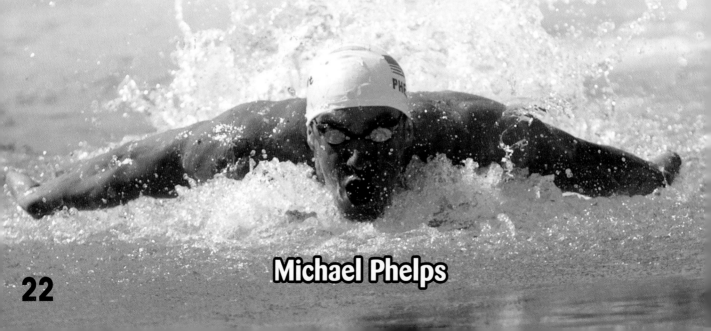

Michael Phelps

Glossary

athlete (AATH-leet) Somebody who plays sports.

career (kuh-RIHR) The time somebody spends doing a certain job.

compete (kuhm-PEET) To play to win or beat another person or another team.

free throw (FREE THROH) In basketball, a basket worth one point.

statistic (stuh-TIHS-tihk) A fact or a piece of data taken from a set of numbers.

touchdown (TUHCH-down) In football, a six-point score made by carrying or throwing the football over the goal line.

Index

Due to the changing nature of Internet links, The Rosen Publishing Group, Inc., has developed an online list of websites related to the subject of this book. This site is updated regularly. Please use this link to access the list: www.powerkidslinks.com/mm/nobt/ssn